MINDFUL MEDITATIONS
for Every Day

SISTER STAN

First published in 2016 by Columba Press
23 Merrion Square
Dublin 2
Ireland
www.columba.ie

ISBN: 978-1-78218-309-9

Set in Tisa Pro 9/14 and Essonnes Display
Book design by Helene Pertl | Columba Press
Printed with Jellyfish Solutions

Front cover image by Matt Hoffman from unsplash.com

MINDFUL MEDITATIONS
for Every Day

SISTER STAN

CONTENTS

CONTENTS

I hope this little book will bring you a greater understanding of how you have been blessed and will sow new seeds of hope and gratitude in your heart.

HOW TO USE THIS BOOK

In this book I have drawn on various translations of scripture and I suggest you use whichever translation appeals to you. I'm suggesting that each month you memorise the scripture quotations, allowing them to sink into your mind and heart.

I suggest that each day you carve out 5–10 minutes for prayer, meditation and reflection. Sit with the scripture in silence. Listen to the voice of the Spirit speaking to you in your heart, in and through the silence. Silence helps the mind to sink into the heart and only in our hearts do we meet God.

The mindful practices for each month may help you to be more centred and to find stillness in your day. You may wish to use these before you enter meditation.

Next, read the thought for the day. These thoughts are only meant to prompt your reflections. Notice what emerges and write your own thought for the day.

It may help you to keep a journal of these reflections as a way of looking back at the end of the day, week, month or year, learning what God is saying to you.

January

STILLNESS

MINDFULNESS FOR JANUARY

Mindfully Waking
Each morning when you wake, before you get out of bed, bring your attention to your breathing. Observe five mindful breaths.

Mindfully Stopping
Each day stop for one minute three times and breath mindfully.

SCRIPTURE FOR JANUARY

Be still and know that I am God.
Psalm 46:10

The peace of God that surpasses all understanding will
guard your hearts and your thoughts in Christ Jesus.
Philippians 4:7

And he arose, and rebuked the wind, and said unto the
sea, 'Peace, be still'.
Mark 4:39

Jesus led them up a high mountain where they could be
alone and there in their presence he was transfigured
before them.
Matthew 17:1–2

1

In the depth of our being there is an inner sanctuary, a secret place guarded by God's presence; we can always go there to be and listen.

2

Through our stillness we can access the beauty within us.

3

The stillness within is a dynamic force, tranquil at its core, that allows us to live fully.

4

Stopping to be still, to listen, helps us recognise God amid the complexities of our lives.

5

In the stillness of our being, wisdom guides us to embrace difficult tasks previously unknown or unacceptable to us.

6

In stillness we embrace our fears and discover a great hidden beauty within us waiting to be explored.

7

To access the stillness at the centre of our being we all need to find a pathway.

8

Each day we can reclaim new areas of peace and stillness within us.

9

When we take time each day to stop, to shut out the busyness of our day, we discover a clarity and a wisdom of which we weren't aware.

10

Silence and stillness appear useless to those who don't experience them; opening ourselves to what may appear useless, we see things as they really are.

11

When we fail to stop and reflect, we lose the signposts that lead us to the sheer joy of living.

12

An overactive life without space for stillness can do violence to ourselves, to our homes, to our families, to our communities.

13

When we take the time to listen to the small voice within, we are brought back to where we are most deeply ourselves.

14

An invitation to stillness is rooted in an undeniable spiritual gravity that allows all things to rest, to settle, to find their place.

15

A frantic, busy life muddies the water of our inner wisdom and understanding. When we rest and still the mind, we experience a new energy and a gradual clarity of perception.

16

The practice of resting in the stillness of our being allows us to delight in life and savour the gifts of all creation.

17

When we act from a place of stillness, we are more
capable of a right understanding, right judgements,
and right decisions and actions.

18

In stillness, we begin to hear the voice of our intuitive
heart, often drowned by the routine of the day.

19

We read in the Bible that God created the world in
six days; on the seventh day God rested. The ancient
rabbis teach us that on the seventh day God created
tranquillity, peace, serenity and repose. Until the
seventh day creation was unfinished. It was only after
the birth of tranquillity that the circle of creation was
full and complete.

20

Being still is to pause, to be awake, to pay attention to what is.

21

Each time the phone rings *stop* and take three mindful silent breaths; you will find it helps you to be more present to the caller.

22

The stillness within us represents the central quiet core where God dwells in us. At the innermost centre of our being there is a place where we are deeply known and loved by God.

23

The still point is the circle of the loving embrace of God.

24

Still points grow and deepen with practice; they are the backbone for a calm, serene life.

25

Finding still points in our day does not mean evading responsibility; it is moving in to life and its responsibilities in a new way.

26

Still points are endless. What you should do during those times is very simple: stop what you are doing, whether sitting or standing, and take a deep breath, with your eyes open or closed, maybe on a bus, a train or a plane, or in the kitchen, or office. Focus your attention inward and simply notice and observe your breathing.

27

The poet Rainer Maria Rilke talks about the importance of stillness. He says, in *The Book of Hours*, 'I am the rest between two notes,' that brief measured moment between the time when one note of music stops and another begins. Without that rest the music would be a chaotic racket. We too need rest and stillness between the activities (notes) of our day, if our life is not to be chaotic.

28

Henry David Thoreau went into the woods to find silence. Writing about his experience, he says, 'I have grown in those seasons like a corn in the night.' We can imagine what it would be like to be inside a cornstalk, inside a growing ear, absorbing the nutrients from the earth. Silently. This is how we grow in the stillness. It happens on its own. We don't have to do anything.

29

Lao Tzu wrote, 'The way to do is to be.' Still point is to do nothing, yet to increase our awareness and remember who we are.

30

Silence is the bridge to ourselves.

31

We all need to discover our own unique paths to stillness. The opportunities are everywhere: in the falling snow, setting sun, growing grass, turning wheel, in our own breath.

February

PRAYER

MINDFULNESS FOR FEBRUARY

....

Mindfully in your body
Each day notice changes in your posture.

Be aware of how your body and mind feel when you move from sitting to standing to walking.

Notice each time you make a transition from one position to the next.

SCRIPTURE FOR FEBRUARY

. . . .

My heart and soul cry out for joy to the living God.
Psalm 84:2

But when you pray, go into your private room, shut the door and pray to your God who is in that secret place.
Matthew 6:6

One day Jesus was praying in a certain place. When he finished one of his disciples said to him, 'Lord teach us to pray, as John taught his disciples.' Jesus said to them, 'When you pray, this is what to say: Father, may your name be held holy, your kingdom come; give us each day our daily bread, and forgive us our sins, for we ourselves forgive each one who is in debt to us. And do not put us to the test.'
Luke 11:1–4

Do you not know that you are God's temple and that God's spirit dwells in you?
1 Corinthians 3:16

1

Prayer helps us move towards a simpler, deeper and more authentic life in which the experience of God is energising and centring.

2

Saints and mystics always met God as a lover, never as a judge or dictator.

3

God, who is at the centre of all that is, calls us to listen to His voice at the centre of our being.

4

Prayer is the letting go of everything that keeps us from the mystery of God in our lives.

5

In prayer, we touch into our deep inner freedom and
our deepest compassion and generosity.

6

Prayer is being in touch with what Yeats calls 'our deep
heart core'.

7

In prayer, we have a sense of union with a presence
beyond us and an overwhelming sense of limitless
belonging.

8

Prayer is finding the divine everywhere: in noise and in
quiet, in light and dark, in the poetic and the mundane,
in the play of children and in the faces of older people,
in the laughter of the carefree and the disappointed
eyes of excluded and oppressed people.

9

Prayer is never achieved. It is the divine taking possession of us and is always a gift.

10

Prayer is the lifting of our hearts, souls, minds and bodies to God, who transforms every aspect of our lives.

11

In prayer, God gazes on us with the creative and transforming eye of love.

12

The great Christian mystic Teresa of Avila describes prayer as noticing God noticing us. It is being attentive, being aware, being alive to what is.

13

Prayer is attentiveness; it is tuning in, listening to and responding to the music of the universe.

14

In prayer, there is no pretence, no control, no sham, just being ourselves.

15

Prayer is being in the present moment, in the now that transcends time.

16

In prayer, there is only a screen between the past and the future. Now is not in time at all. Now is beyond time.

17

In prayer, we encounter God breathing gently on us with great tenderness.

18

To pray is to allow the child within us to come into its own, ready to be surprised by God.

19

Prayer never excludes, always an inclusive communion with God and others.

20

To be prayerful people we need to develop the habit of prayer: a disciplined practice of prayer that flows over into our whole life – then all our life is prayer.

21

. . . .

True prayer is never a private matter. It is a way of life that changes the way we think and shapes the way we live.

22

. . . .

To become a prayerful person we need time and space for silence and solitude so we can commune with God.

23

. . . .

Prayer is resting in God.

24

. . . .

In prayer, we face the winter of our life, as we lie quiet and fallow for a while, knowing that only in the quiet and stillness can we hear the tiny whispers of new life.

25

Interior prayer is moving beyond ourselves to be transformed into divine love.

26

Prayer is joyful acceptance of life's great gifts.

27

Prayer is living from the heart.

28

You keep those in perfect peace whose mind is fixed on you because they trust in you forever, for you are our God, our everlasting rock.

Isaiah 26:3–4

March

HOPE

MINDFULNESS FOR MARCH

. . . .

Mindfully Breathing

Remember to connect with your breath and body throughout the day, and at regular times each day stop, bring your attention to your breathing and observe five mindful breaths.

SCRIPTURE FOR MARCH

Praise be to God the Father of our Lord Jesus Christ! In his great mercy he has given us new birth by raising Jesus Christ from the dead so that we have a sure hope that will never fade away.

1 Peter 1:4

May the God of hope fill you with joy and peace and may you abound in hope.

Romans 15:13

'For I know the plans I have for you,' says the Lord. 'They are plans for good and not for disaster, to give you a future and a hope.'

Jeremiah 29:11

For I am convinced that neither death nor life, neither angels nor princes, neither the present nor the future, nor any powers, neither height nor depth, nor anything else in all creation, will be able to separate us from the love of God made visible in Christ Jesus our Lord.

Romans 8:38–39

1

Hope belongs in the realm of ongoing mystery, the human endeavour that penetrates the darkness and the realities around us.

2

It is easy to lose hope when we lose touch with our sources and allow daily routines to rule our lives.

3

The seed of God is within us, wanting to grow, therefore we cannot settle or rest except in God.

4

St Augustine says that hope has two daughters: anger and courage. They enable us to do remarkable things and make possible what we want to happen in the future.

5

Hope lives on the edge between the near and the far, the finite and the infinite, the now and the not yet. It is believing what is not yet and seeing what is not yet visible.

6

Hope is trusting what is happening will eventually make sense or if it never makes sense it will still offer an opportunity for growth.

7

Hope assures us each morning that our life is of value no matter how unsettling or disturbing our current situation may be.

8

Hope encourages us not to give up when it is time to move on.

9

Hope accepts mystery and trusts the unknown.

10

Hope doesn't pretend that we will get all we want or that there won't be trouble along the way but it promises growth with the struggle.

11

Hope is discovering the truth about ourselves in the midst of darkness.

12

Hope is accepting our mortality when we encounter our physical weakness.

13

Hope is living our dreams even when we experience failure and doubt.

14

We all carry the fire of hope in our hearts but we need to rekindle it. This fire gives us the courage to believe in the dreams that stir in our souls.

15

Hope is learning the one important lesson in life: how to begin again.

16

Hope is when we refuse to take the beauty of a flower for granted.

17

Hope is not optimism; it is what we have when the bottom falls out of optimism.

18

Hope is seeing the reality of despair in the world and yet seeing that all is in tune with the divine purpose of creation.

19

True hope sees beyond the imaginable. It is divine. It is our call to what is not yet.

20

To hope is to experience a power and a presence that is greater than we are and to experience it when we do not see it.

21

Treasured memories can sustain us in hope, even in times of great trouble and suffering.

22

Hope has the audacity to reach a hand into darkness and come out with a handful of light.

23

Hope is waiting with resilience in the certain knowledge that if we wait long enough and if we are true to ourselves things will make sense.

24

Hope is to believe in the transformation of society even in the midst of great oppression when nothing seems to improve or change.

25

Hope is believing there is beauty and meaning in our lives, right up to the end. When we let go, hope expands.

26

Our capacity for hope can diminish when there is no room for miracles or mystery.

27

Hope is bold in the face of sickness, grief, loneliness, even poverty and misery.

28

Hope is about what is not yet, what we do not see but trust is there.

29

Hope is daring to let God be God.

30

To be a person of hope is to be willing to move out and sit at the edge of our fear, our anger, our grief, rather than being controlled by it.

31

Being a person of hope means waiting without being afraid of the dark, the silence, the emptiness. It is in the emptiness, the darkness and the nothingness that hope is brought forth.

April

WONDER

MINDFULNESS FOR APRIL

. . . .

Mindful Walking
Pay attention to your body walking; notice your
posture.

Pay attention to your body while you walk; notice the
contact of your feet with the ground.

Feel the air on your face, arms and legs as you walk.

SCRIPTURE FOR APRIL

. . . .

Everyone was gripped with great wonder and awe, and
they praised God, exclaiming, 'We have seen amazing
things today!'

Luke 5:26

Many, Lord my God,
are the wonders you have done,
the things you planned for us.
None can compare with you;
were I to speak and tell of your deeds,
they would be too many to declare.

Psalm 40:5

For it was you who created my being,
knit me together in my mother's womb.
I thank you for the wonder of my being,
for the wonders of all your creation.

Psalm 139:13–14

Those who dwell in the earth's farthest bounds
stand in awe at your wonders.
You make the sunrise and the sunset
shout for joy.

Psalm 65:8

1

We need reminders to focus our attention on the wonders of life and to say, with Patrick Kavanagh, we are able to find 'a star lovely-art, in a dark sod'.

2

'Let me so walk upon you that even though you must bend your head under my feet as I pass by you will know after I am gone that I am your sister.'
Native American prayer for the grass

3

To appreciate the wonder all around us we must get out of our own way, out of our own light.

4

We must realise that the earth does not belong to us, that we belong to the earth; we are part of the earth and she is part of us.

5

The earth speaks to us when we listen with our hearts; it speaks the language of love, in the shape of a new leaf, the feel of a worn stone, the colour of the evening sky, the smell of summer rain, the sound of the night wind.

6

The earth's whispers are everywhere; only those who have slept and dreamt with it can respond to it.

7

The earth speaks in magic – magical rainbows, waterfalls, interacting sunlight and air and water and soil – creating a constantly shifting rich kaleidoscope.

8

Today, lift a fistful of earth and give thanks to the life it sustains. Today, bend down and touch the grass, greet the first tree you meet this morning. Today, listen to the rain.

9

We may have listened for too long to the voices of one form of life, forgetting that we share this earth also with multitudes of other life.

10

We need to rebuild our relationship with the earth, to hear the earth's song, to know its harmony and realise its connection with us.

11

Our questions offer us possibilities for new things; when we stay with our questions, insight is born.

12

Seeing with the eyes of the heart is seeing, beyond the senses and beneath the surface, to the sacredness of life.

13

Every rainbow is an invitation to stop, to stare, to wonder.

14

The world waits each day for us to greet it with wonderment.

15

If we see everyone as special and interesting, the world will be a fascinating place for us.

16

When we choose to surrender to surprise, we are more in control of our lives.

17

Stay awake to the possibilities of each moment; anticipating the future robs us of surprise.

18

We discover the beauty and wonder of our life just by living deliberately.

19

No one can enter into the uniqueness of our experience of wonder, even those closest to us.

20

Surprise is what encourages us to relate to the world
with a sense of wonder.

21

Life unfolds in mystery and our journey into mystery
is guided by the inner light of faith at the core of our
being, whether we are aware of it or not.

22

In wonderment we lose ourselves, we are emptied of
our little selves and we realise how wonderful the world
is and how full of wonder it is.

23

When we stop and take time for silence and solitude we
learn to be attentive, a prerequisite for wonderment.

24

When we pay attention to everything we hear, see, smell, taste and touch, we will be constantly moved, surprised, amazed and be in a state of wonder and awe.

25

Time spent in solitude and silence helps us to slow down in the midst of our busy lives, not necessarily so that we do less, but so that we do what we do more attentively, more reverently, more leisurely and with wonderment.

26

Wonderment is not the privilege of those who have time. It is the virtue and wisdom of those who take time to live attentively and take things as they come, one by one, singling out each person, place, experience and situation and living them to the full.

27

The virtues of attentiveness enable us to witness the wonders of the journey despite our concerns with the destination, the result, the product.

28

May I seed my days with golden moments of silence, stillness and wonderment.

29

Awareness is the essence of wonder. In the Zen tradition, there is a story that goes like this: a disciple asks his master, 'Could there be anything more wonderful than the beauty of creation?' For a long time the master was silent, then he responded, 'Indeed there is.' 'What can this be?' the disciple asked. The master answered, 'Your own present awareness of the wonder and beauty of creation.'

To be interiorly aware is to be in a state of reverential appreciation and wonderment.

May

WISDOM

MINDFULNESS FOR MAY

....

Mindful Eating

Before you eat something take a minute and breathe;
look at your food and give thanks.

Imagine that you have never seen this food before and
you don't know what it is.

Use all your senses: seeing, hearing, touching, smelling
and tasting to experience this food.

Think of the journey this food has made to be here, and
give thanks.

SCRIPTURE FOR MAY

The mouths of the righteous utter wisdom,
and their tongues speak justice.
The law of their God is in their hearts;
their steps do not slip.

Psalm 37:30–31

Listen to me: be silent, and I will teach you wisdom.

Job 33:33

And Jesus increased in wisdom, in stature, and in
favour with God and man.

Luke 2:52

All that came into being in him was life, life that was
the light of men, a light that shines in the dark, a light
that darkness could not overpower.

John 1:4–5

1

Look into your heart today and choose one action that will change your heart and ultimately the world.

2

Accepting people we meet as they are keeps our hearts open to wisdom.

3

Wisdom is the reward for a lifetime of listening.

4

When we see with the heart and listen with the soul, we find a new way of being.

5

Wisdom comes when we celebrate and accept what we have and rejoice in the present, not thinking of what is past, or what might have been or will be. The time of wisdom is now.

6

Wisdom is to celebrate ourselves: to accept ourselves as we are with our gifts, abilities, shortcomings, inner wounds, darkness, mortality and knowing that it is what gives our lives direction and meaning.

7

The harvest time of our lives is a time to gather all the experiences of our lives, celebrate them and share that with friends and neighbours.

8

At the harvest time of our lives we can be mentors, people of grace and wisdom, that younger people love to be around.

9

Being honest about our struggles and fears and hopes is the best gift we can pass on to others.

10

Each one of us has his or her secret or mystery, his or her particular journey, his or her vocation to grow. Spending time in this knowing place, we realise our fruitfulness and can reap and share our harvest of wisdom.

11

Wisdom is the opposite of being obsessed with achievement and success. The wise person works out of love with no assurance of success, considers trying more important than achieving, questions more important than answers.

12

Wisdom has more to do with being than with doing, being fruitful rather than achieving success. Being fruitful means becoming each day more and more what we are called to be.

13

The wise person moves from challenge to challenge with a trusting soul, with hope and joy, always ready to begin again.

14

To leap in the dark is to take the risk that this moment is the right moment to do what we must do. Henry David Thoreau says 'We must walk consciously only part way towards our goal and then leap in the dark to our success.'

15

To see with the heart is to see with awareness of life's deepest meanings.

16

Gratitude brings a wisdom that enables us to walk unafraid into unknown places, knowing we are loved and blessed.

17

To truly listen to our wisdom we have to empty ourselves of ourselves.

18

Wisdom is walking mindfully in a garden with a three-year-old, noticing everything the child notices.

19

To grow in wisdom we have to stay connected with the source of love and inspiration, the source of our life.

20

If we are moving at great speed, every delay is seen as a personal affront. If, on the other hand, we choose to slow down and surrender to surprise, we will find we are much more relaxed and in control of life.

21

At the centre of our being there is a core of truth. This is what compels us to follow our conscience, to put ourselves on the line no matter what the consequences may be.

22

We may never be able to see how our actions affect the world but with faith and wisdom we know we matter.

23

Surrendering ourselves to the possibility of something new and unknown will give us a resilience to whatever life may offer.

24

Wisdom is lived in reciprocal relationships of giving and receiving, trusting that our contribution affects many whether we are aware of it or not.

25

Wisdom comes from God in prayer but is also available through the ordinary events of daily life.

26

A true mark of wisdom is humility; it is seeing the extraordinary in the ordinary.

27

To see with wisdom does not change the difficulty of the problem but it changes the depth of our understanding and the quality of our response.

28

It is what is deepest within us and not what is happening around us that determines the quality of our lives.

29

Each of us is responsible for our inner life and the more we fill it with thoughts of goodness, generosity, peace and love, the happier and wiser we are and the better the quality of our lives.

30

True wisdom is knowing that the happiness that we seek is already within us.

31

It is a strange paradox: the more we forget ourselves the more we find our true selves.

June

BEAUTY

MINDFULNESS FOR JUNE

....

Mindful Listening

Bring your awareness to your listening. Try to listen
with attention, without agreeing or disagreeing, liking
or disliking, or planning what you will say in response.

When speaking, try to say what you need to say without
exaggeration and notice how your mind and body feels.

SCRIPTURE FOR JUNE

Consider the lilies of the field, how they grow: they neither toil nor spin, yet I tell you, even Solomon in all his glory was not arrayed like one of these.

Matthew 6:28–29

We are God's work of art, created in Christ Jesus to live the good life as from the beginning he has meant us to live it.

Ephesians 2:10

One thing I ask from the Lord,
    this only do I seek:
that I may dwell in the house of the Lord
    all the days of my life,
to gaze on the beauty of the Lord,
    to seek him in his temple.

Psalm 27:4

You shall be a crown of beauty in the hand of the Lord.

Isaiah 62:3

Art makes visible the visible

1

Beauty is a beacon in our mind that brings us home to our best selves.

2

2022

Beauty brings us to the realisation that in the midst of our struggles and in the depths of darkness the best in life is possible.

3

Paul Klee says, 'Art does not reproduce the visible; rather, it makes visible.'

4

Beauty is a call to every soul to come to life and see, and rise to the heights of itself.

5

John Cassian writes, 'The highest spiritual intention is one of contemplating beauty.'

6

We cannot hope for fullness of life without nurturing fullness of soul.

7

The beauty we nourish within ourselves creates a beautiful world.

8

When we stay with the familiar, the controlled version of ourselves, the great mystery and beauty of our being never emerges and is unknown ever to ourselves.

9

The journey of self-knowledge and self-acceptance is a journey to find our true selves, the great mystery of who we are.

10

We are born to make known the great wonder and glory of God that is within the hearts of each of us.

11

Each dawn a new genesis, a new beginning, a resurrection, a new beauty is born. Each day we are invited to search and seek who we are called to be.

12

The more we let go of our ego the more we allow the unknown true self to emerge.

13

At the precise point when we accept our own weakness and fragility, true development and growth takes place.

14

Change begins in the dark when we accept that we are not complete.

15

When we accept that part of us is fragmented, we discover the source of our growth and our true beauty.

16

The fullness and brightness of God is still at the centre of our being.

17

When we are truly human and truly ourselves, it is God's glory that shines through us.

18

We can create beauty and wonder in our lives just by living.

19

If we dare to risk we will discover something we never dreamed of.

20

When we stop and listen to our deepest selves, we hear the voice of God.

21

Simplicity frees us from false values that rate possession or striving above all else.

22

Simplicity opens us to receiving the beauty of the moment, the joy of the day.

23

When we simplify our lives, we open our hearts to emptiness, where fullness becomes possible.

24

The infinite beauty of God begins with the gift of life itself and continues with everything that sustains it.

25

We are known by our creator God in a depth and fullness and beauty of our being that surpasses all our dreams, hopes and imagination.

26

Painting the landscape calls us to be still in its beauty.

27

There are moments in our lives when we are called to stand at the edge, where the possibilities before us are immense, the challenges mighty. These moments call for creativity, courage and hope.

28

If our life is not about truth and beauty and goodness then our creative energies are destroying not creating. Life is simple and serene, full of joy, peace and beauty when it is lived from the heart. A daily miracle: a flower opens to morning light, it closes fast its petals as light fades.

29

The darkness before dawn is pregnant with beautiful light.

30

Everything in nature yearns: weeds pushing through pavements, baby birds calling for food. So our souls yearn for divine beauty.

July

LOVE

MINDFULNESS FOR JULY

. . . .

Mindful Waiting
When waiting, bring your attention to your breathing.

If you notice any impatience bring your attention back to your breathing in the present moment.

Feel the contact of your feet in your shoes on the floor.

Feel the rise and fall of your abdomen.

SCRIPTURE FOR JULY

If we love one another, God lives in us, and his love is perfected in us.

1 John 4:12

Love is patient and kind. Love is not jealous or boastful or proud or rude. It does not demand its own way. It is not irritable, and it keeps no record of being wronged. Love does not rejoice about injustice but rejoices whenever the truth wins out.

1 Corinthians 13:4–6

I shall remove the heart of stone from your bodies and give you a heart of flesh instead.

Ezekiel 36:26

The fruit of the spirit is love, joy, peace, patience, kindness, goodness, faithfulness, gentleness and self-control. Against such things there is no law.

Galatians 5:22

1

Our incomplete nature yearns and springs towards its own perfection and we cannot rest until we find the true source of that perfection.

2

Deep within each of us there is a fountain of love; the greatest gift we can offer another is to reveal to them that hidden reservoir of love.

3

The heart stands at the centre of my being, where I am at one with myself, at one with others and at one with the pure spirit of God.

4

When we open up to people their ability to love, we are doing the work of God; we are freeing people in a way they didn't know.

5

We have an infinite capacity for love; God's love within us remains undeveloped if we don't use it.

6

Human love as we know it is a glimpse of the eternal love of God. True love is heartbreaking, breathtaking; it is God's love made visible on earth.

7

Through love, we can reach and see beyond ourselves, connecting us to the rest of the world and freeing us from ourselves.

8

Each day I am shaped and reshaped by my reception of the relationships, events and experiences of the day.

9

Behind my ordinary daily life lies an extraordinary mystery unexplored, extraordinary potential unrealised, extraordinary beauty unknown.

10

We stand at the edge of our unknown selves. We must stand aside and let the unknown, unloved stranger in us emerge.

11

A loving heart brings peace, joy, harmony and beauty.

12

The desire to perform great acts of heroism or good may stifle the small daily acts of kindness.

13

The deepest desire of the human heart is to belong.

14

Jesus is the revelation of the heart of God.

15

A flame of love lies in the heart of everyone.

16

What we love shapes our lives.

17

Our full attention is the greatest gift we can give one another.

18

Happiness comes from loving ourselves as we are.

19

No good action is a private matter; every good action makes the world a better place.

20

Love begins in the heart and is reinforced and enhanced with every act of kindness.

21

Indifference towards another is the greatest offence we can offer them.

22

Apathy can be a most destructive force, robbing us of life.

23

No loving thought, word or deed escapes its effect.

24

Fear can prevent us from being a person of courage and love. If we allow the love in us to take over it will carry us forward without fear.

25

Simple acts of kindness give our lives meaning.

26

True love need not be earned;
it is there whether we respond to it or not.

27

When we love, we recognise a depth in the presence of the other that cannot be seen or found without love.

28

The most ordinary actions can be a kindness if we do them with love.

29

Love transforms the most horrific situations into beauty and light.

30

Only God's love is perfect and unconditional. Human love can only approximate that love but if we consent to it and give ourselves over to its fullness, the entire world will be overflowing with love.

31

Every mountain teaches us silence; every flower teaches us impermanency; every ocean teaches us peace; love always teaches us love.

August

GRATITUDE

MINDFULNESS FOR AUGUST

....

Mindful in activities
Choose a simple daily activity, perhaps brushing your teeth or washing your hands, and see if you can bring your full attention to what you are doing, the sensations involved, the subtle movements. Notice where your mind is as you do this and gently bring it back to what you are doing if it has wandered.

SCRIPTURE FOR AUGUST

....

What return shall I make to God
    for all God's bounty to me?
I will lift up the cup of salvation
    and call on the name of God.
Psalm 116:12–13

And may the peace of Christ reign in your hearts,
because it is for this that you were called together in
one body. Always be thankful.
Colossians 3:15

Blessed be the God and Father of our Lord Jesus Christ,
the merciful Father and the God who gives every
possible encouragement.
2 Corinthians 1:3–4

Glory to God whose power, working in us, can do
infinitely more than we can ask or imagine; glory be to
him from generation to generation in the Church and
in Christ Jesus for ever and ever. Amen.
Ephesians 3:20–21

1

When we live with gratitude, dreams become possible,
sorrows and losses bearable.

2

Gratitude is not just a feeling – it is not enough to feel
grateful. We must think gratefully, imagine gratefully
and act gratefully.

3

When we search for reasons to be grateful we find they
are endless. If we open our eyes to see and our ears to
hear and our heart to feel, we will find gifts all around
us and within us.

4

When we face life with the eye of gratefulness, with
a sense of receiving rather than taking, everything
changes.

5

Life is a gift and as with all gifts we are called to live it in gratitude.

6

The greatest gift we can give is thanksgiving. In giving gifts we often give what we can spare, but in giving thanks we give ourselves.

7

When we don't take things for granted, we recognise everything is a gift. Even the predictable turns into a surprise when we stop taking it for granted.

8

May I live with an open heart of gratitude, realising that each moment is unique.

9

When we consent to live deliberately in the present, without looking to the past or to the future, we realise this moment is the only one we are sure of.

10

When we see life with gratitude, we realise that there is nothing too small, mundane, ecstatic, exalted, ordinary or extraordinary that doesn't contain surprise.

11

All of life is full of potential; all of life is full of surprises. May I recognise and accept the greatness of each person and meet them with a fresh gaze and an open heart.

12

When we accept that a part of us is still incomplete, still fragmented, that part becomes the source of our growth.

13

When we realise that each year, each day, each moment is a gift, we realise that life is not about the length of years; rather, it is about living into the opportunity offered in each moment with gratitude.

14

When we see our older age as a new stage in life, we let go of the fantasies of staying young and the fears of getting older and find the beauty and happiness of each day.

15

When we are grateful, we realise that our life is a series of moments, each of them new, each of them with their own purpose.

16

Each moment has its own task, its own potential and possibilities designed to lead us to happiness, fulfilment and gratitude.

17

Gratitude is like the sun lighting up the landscape: not a single leaf or blade of grass is different but everything looks much more beautiful.

18

Let each day begin and close with thanksgiving.

19

'I am so happy, so happy.
I loved my life.'
Gerard Manley Hopkins, on his deathbed

20

Today, may I dwell with gratitude on the mystery of my being and take nothing for granted.

21

Genuine gratitude comes from the heart, where we are rooted in love.

22

Often it is the difficulties of life that open us to gratitude, the difficulties ease when gratitude begins.

23

Humility helps us to realise we are one among many mortal and limited human beings.

24

The dance of life is totally dependent on the constant exchange of giving and receiving.

25

....

Gratitude helps us to keep perspective and make connections that might otherwise be overlooked.

26

....

The more we are aware of the unity and oneness of all life, the more we are aware that nothing is ours alone but we hold everything in trust and are grateful.

27

....

When we see ourselves as we really are, we cannot judge or condemn another person.

28

....

'For all that has been, thank you.
For all that is to come, yes.'
   Dag hammarskjöld

29

'If the only prayer we ever said was "thank you" it would be enough.'

Meister Eckhart

30

The one who says 'thank you' to another really says 'we belong together'. The giver and thanks giver belong to each other.

31

Gratitude is at the heart of a healthy spirituality. When we are grateful, our lives begin to change instantly and we will see we have much more than we previously realised.

September

LIFE TO THE FULL

MINDFULNESS FOR SEPTEMBER

. . . .

Mindfully Moving
Your body is always present but the mind is often elsewhere. As you sit reading this, notice the sensations in your body at this moment.

When you have finished reading, stand and feel the movement of standing, noticing how the body feels with even the smallest movement.

Be in your body as you move, as you reach out, as you turn. Be present.

SCRIPTURE FOR SEPTEMBER

. . . .

I am the light of the world; anyone who follows me will
not be walking in the dark but will have the light of life.

John 8:12

It is the spirit that gives life, the flesh has nothing to
offer. The words I have spoken to you are spirit and
they are life.

John 6:63

I am the resurrection. Anyone who believes in me, even
though that person dies, will live, and whoever lives
and believes in me will never die.

John 11:25–26

I have come that you may have life and have it to the full.

John 10:10

1

The incarnation of God in Jesus is meaningless to us if we do not allow God to come alive in us.

2

When we experience the interconnectedness of all things, we are suddenly awakened to the sacred vitality of all forms of life.

3

We are interconnected across time and eternity; there is an eternal region within us. Medieval English mystic Julian of Norwich described it thus, 'God never began to love us, God has loved us for all eternity, we were all born into each other.'

4

Eckhart talks about the spiritual life as 'coming home to your soul to the house you never left'.

5

We are interconnected not only here and now, in this time and this space, but with everything in the past and in the future and into the unknown dimensions of all eternity. Oscar Wilde said, 'We think in eternity but we move slowly through time.'

6

When we are awake, we feel the breeze caressing our skin, we sense the leaves rustling in the wind, notice the morning dew drawing the spider's web, see the night give way to day and seasons give way to seasons.

7

To live fully is to be a sower. The sower knows the secret of growth, the slow process that needs its own time, waiting for life to emerge. The life-giver releases the beauty and potential hidden within.

8

The sower marvels to see the power of life pushing up the buds from the earth. That marvel repeats itself spring after spring after spring. Even though it is exactly what is expected to happen, it is always a surprise to see the soil responding to the sun above and the moisture below, to see the blades of grass pushing up through the soil, the plant strengthening and growing, the crop thickening on the stem and the fruit swelling on the branches.

9

Life unfolds everywhere at its own pace. It cannot be rushed. It happens in its own time.

10

Living life to the full is believing that there is a time for everything. Our task is to carry out our work without ceasing, never knowing where the seed will grow, never quitting, always waiting in hope.

11

The sower is not concerned with himself, his life is lived
at the edge, planting the questions and possibilities
in human hearts, never knowing what effect they will
have. He is prepared to live with the questions.

12

The sowers have a vision and though they may fail and
fail again, they try and try again, and in their trying
they are beacon lights of hope for many.

13

Everything has a time; our time is now. To live our lives
every minute, every hour, every day, every year. Now is
the time to live the lives we have been gifted with.

14

Life is for living; we can miss it and let it pass us by if we
are unwilling to engage with it in the present.

15

Life is not a consumer good that needs to be grasped and used. We cannot cage life: we cannot freeze it. It moves on, it races, it limps, it reaches highs, it sinks to lows, sometimes it appears too slow, other times too fast. All we are asked is to live it moment by moment.

16

The real measure of life is not whether we have lived the length of our days but whether we have lived the depth and breadth of them.

17

We cannot reduce life to our size; what we can do is explore and drink deep each moment. Accept, acknowledge, rejoice in every experience and learn from every single moment.

18

Life is not what happens outside us; life is what is happening inside us. It happens through us, because of us and in spite of us.

19

There is no such thing as a meaningless moment or a meaningless life. If we are open to it, life will teach and enable us to become people of wisdom, compassion and joy, in our age and in our time.

20

If we are open and awake to life, the cycle of time shapes and reshapes us until we become who we are called to be.

21

When we are authentically and fully in touch with ourselves, we experience God.

22

We limit our lives by thoughtless daily repetition.

23

Brendan Kennelly said, 'How easy it is to maim the moment with expectations, to force it to define itself.' We live with one foot in tomorrow and miss the very richness of the present moment.

24

This is my time right here, right now, in this spot, this village, this town, this city. What happens here and now is my responsibility.

25

Life is not a matter of doing great things; it is a matter of doing or saying small things with care, responsibility and courage.

26

When we have done what we must do, what we were put here to do, in this time and this place, we are who we are called to be and nobody can take that from us. However hard life may be, however difficult the tests and pressures, even if we appear to fail and people leave us and reject us and disown us, we will never die before we have lived our lives to the full.

27

Life offers us choices. Freedom to choose is one of life's greatest gift. We can choose to believe that lessons can be learned from the worst situations, and growth is always possible.

28

When we are generous to someone, the boundaries between us become more porous.

29

. . . .

We need not take responsibility for others; rather, we must be responsible *to* them and *for* ourselves.

30

. . . .

Whenever we give a gift, it is essential that at the moment of giving we also give ourselves.

October

FREEDOM

MINDFULNESS FOR OCTOBER

Mindfully Sitting

Take five minutes each day to sit tall, with your feet
on the floor, your back straight, shoulders relaxed, the
head resting gently on the neck and shoulders; just sit,
relaxed, and be still.

Be aware of your surroundings – your body, the sounds
around you. Don't change anything, just be aware.
Finish with five mindful breaths.

SCRIPTURE FOR OCTOBER

. . . .

Now this Lord is the Spirit and where the Spirit of the
Lord is, there is freedom.

2 Corinthians 3:17

You, my brothers and sisters, were called to be free,
serve one another humbly in love. For the entire law
is fulfilled in keeping this one command: 'Love your
neighbour as yourself.'

Galatians 5:13–14

It is for freedom that Christ has set us free. Stand firm,
then, and do not let yourselves be burdened again by
yoke of slavery.

Galatians 5:1

The Spirit of the Lord is upon me, because the Lord
has anointed me to bring good news to the poor; he
has sent me to bind up the brokenhearted, to proclaim
liberty to the captives, freedom to those in prison, to
proclaim a year of favour from Yahweh and a day of
vengeance for our God.

Isaiah 61:1–2

1

When we have the courage to confront our deep secret fears, we will be free.

2

Every time we trust, we put ourselves on the line. Trust costs us but it is worth it.

3

Knowing and claiming the past helps us free the future.

4

If we look for the unexpected and see our lives with openness, we will hear the small voice within and be surprised.

5

Everyone yearns for something to live for, the key to finding it is the courage and zest we develop on our journey.

6

We live in a changing world; if we don't change, we perish.

7

When we accept our limitations, we experience a new freedom.

8

Trust is the keeper of relationships.

9

As long as there are people in the world who don't have enough, there is always an opportunity to share.

10

What word is waiting to be set free in us today.

11

To rediscover the art of waiting and to teach it to our children is to give them one of the world's greatest and best possible gifts.

12

'If you want others to be happy, practise compassion. If you want to be happy, practise compassion.'
   His Holiness, the Dalai Lama

13

Life is created when we trust in the promise of unseen things, just as buds hold life in the depth of darkness.

14

Every war is within us and only you and I can stop what causes the war.

15

Every frightening situation offers us a chance to grow.

16

Our personal transformation affects the whole world.

17

When we change the way we see things, the things we see change.

18

A problem looked at in another way is often its solution.

19

Trust is a dance between what is and what could be.

20

Everything is sacred for those who know how to see.

21

Our shared humanity matters more than our differences.

22

The moment we decide to give away something we treasure to enrich the life of another, we enter a new freedom.

23

When we step outside our inner concerns and worries and enter the world of other people's passions, fears, hopes and suffering, we see our concerns more objectively and are freer and happier.

24

If we devote ourselves to competing with others, we have less energy and inner freedom for what really matters.

25

Our most precious material things, even those we think will endure, are like sandcastles that are swept away when the tide comes in.

26

To surrender does not make us weak, it makes us humble, admitting to ourselves and others that we are not perfect, that we are human and make mistakes.

27

The swallows would never experience their long journeys over sea and land if they hadn't the courage to leave the nest and fly.

28

The greater our awareness of each moment, the more we begin to let go of the stories that control us.

29

Life is a journey; every moment either diminishes or frees us.

30

Life is God's gift to us and what we make of that gift is our gift to God.

31

Our life is no more than a moment in the vast universe of time.

November

SOLITUDE

MINDFULNESS FOR NOVEMBER

. . . .

Mindfully Releasing Tension
Become aware of any tension in your body.

Take a slow deep breath. Breathe into the tightness
and as you exhale release the tension, notice where
you store tension in your body: perhaps in your neck,
shoulders, stomach, jaw and back.

On a regular basis, breathe into those places and as you
exhale notice the tension leaving your body.

With just a few conscious breaths, we release the
tension in our body and mind and return to a state of
calm presence.

SCRIPTURE FOR NOVEMBER

After he had dismissed the crowds he went up the mountain by himself to pray. When evening came, he was there alone.

Matthew 14:23

Jesus withdrew to a lonely place to pray.

Luke 5:16

Jesus went out to a mountainside to pray, and spent the whole night in prayer to God. When day came, he called his disciples to him and chose twelve of them.

Luke 6:12–13

For God alone my soul waits in silence,
for my hope is from Him.

Psalm 62:5

1

Solitude is being alone but not isolated, tuned into ourselves and the world around us.

2

Thomas Merton writes, 'A monk is a marginal person who withdraws deliberately with a view to deepening their fundamental human experience.'

3

Solitude is not a refusal to be involved with the world. In solitude, we carry people in our hearts, experiencing a deep bonding with them even though they are not present.

4

Solitude and silence make us wise because in solitude we come to know ourselves.

5

In solitude, we learn to deal more kindly with ourselves and with others. Knowing our struggles, we can recognise the struggles of others; knowing our frailty and fragility, we are less quick to judge, less certain of our conviction and more open to the goodness of all around us.

6

Loneliness is a painful experience, feeling cut off or excluded. Solitude is an experience of serenity, peace, freedom and inclusion.

7

Time spent in solitude is a time to be, to listen without doing, planning, analysing, theorising or judging. It is a time to be open to the moment, a time to listen with a quiet mind.

8

It is only in solitude and silence we can begin to hear the voice of our intuitive heart, easily drowned out by our busy lives and minds.

9

The mystical writer Herman Hesse writes of the disciple who learned more from listening to the river than to his master. 'He learned from it continually and above all he learned from it how to listen with a still heart, with a waiting, open soul, without passion, without desire, without judgements, without opinions.' We can only learn to listen like this when we are prepared to stop and to be still, to be open, to be empty, to hear the inner stirrings of our heart and the heart of the universe.

10

In silence, we can listen deeply; the more deeply we listen the more we tune into the inner cries of our heart and learn how to respond to them.

11

Only in silence can our conscious minds grasp a tiny fraction of the wonder and reality of our identity as children of God.

12

In solitude and silence, we can enter a deeper level of consciousness of the interrelatedness of all things and the essential unity and eternal harmony of the universe.

13

In silence and solitude, our hearts and minds can be raised to a level of consciousness that we cannot attain in the noise and chatter and clutter of our world.

14

In solitude, we are called beyond the limits of our humanity to see things in their true perspective.

15

A time of solitude is a time of intimacy with ourselves, a time to embrace and befriend ourselves.

16

Solitude creates the conditions to be at home with ourselves.

17

Solitude brings us face-to-face with ourselves, our own inner motivations and compulsions, and forces us to discover a new depth in ourselves.

18

In solitude, we learn to see beyond our frailties and emptiness to a new awareness, leading to acceptance.

19

If we reject ourselves and refuse to say yes to who we are, we impoverish and diminish ourselves. If we accept and embrace who we are, we can make room for the power of love to transform us and radiate through us.

20

In solitude, we discover that deep down inside of us is a microcosm of all the hopes, fears, joys and sorrows, pains and delights of the whole universe.

·21

Silence and solitude enable us to listen beyond the chaos that is inside us and around us, to hear our own unasked questions.

22

In solitude and silence, we can tune ourselves in to the true source of our being, the true source of our identity and security, the source of our life.

23

It is in solitude that we can face and accept, without fear, our own inner poverty and our brokenness, our faults and our frailties, our inadequacies – knowing that in God's embrace we are transformed by a love that has no requirements and no limits.

24

We all need a space for solitude. Once we experience it, we prize the opportunity to stop, be still and at rest with ourselves.

25

The function of silence is not to cut us off from the rest of the world; it is to enable us to listen to what is going on within and without.

26

Solitude deepens our capacity for wonder. When we stop and spend time in solitude, we are wooed into the wonder of creation, the wonder of God.

27

If we make space for solitude and silence in our lives, we can enter a deep knowing within our being.

28

As long as we are full of ourselves, with no empty space for solitude and silence, we are incapable of wonderment and life seems empty.

29

Moments when we can bless and feel blessed are moments when we are most alone, yet most alive to everything and everyone around us.

30

May I seed my days with golden moments of silence and stillness.

December

PEACE

MINDFULNESS FOR DECEMBER

. . . .

Mindfully ending the day
Before going to sleep at night, bring your attention
to your breathing; breathe mindfully, observing the
breath entering and leaving the body.

Spend a few minutes and look back over your day.
Notice times when you were mindful. Reflect on the
people and events of the day.

If your mind wanders, gently bring it back to the
breath.

Continue to review your day.

Give thanks.

SCRIPTURE FOR DECEMBER

....

Peace I leave with you; my peace I give to you; not as the world gives do I give to you. Do not let your heart be troubled or afraid.

John 14:27

The Lord gives strength to his people;
the Lord blesses his people with peace.

Psalm 29:11

For I know the thoughts that I think toward you, says the Lord, thoughts of peace and not of evil, to give you a future and a hope.

Jeremiah 29:11

And if the house be worthy, let your peace come upon it; if it be not worthy, let your peace return to you.

Matthew 10:13

1

We all have shadows that need attention: our fears, our grudges, our memories. The war goes on inside us; only you and I can stop that war.

2

To be people of peace and justice, we must live in our own inner peace.

3

Our task in the world is to cooperate with the creator God in transforming our world into God's reign of justice, peace and love.

4

Being people of peace and building peace in and through our lives challenges the status quo.

5

Forgiveness is an attitude to life, not something we do occasionally.

6

Forgiveness is the key to inner freedom and peace.

7

Peace comes when we plumb our depths, take the measure of ourselves and find the world within us.

meaning ? NOTHING

8

Peacemaking is not passivity, it is creative action that seeks justice.

9

Peace comes when we have met and accepted the best and the worst in ourselves.

10

Peace comes when we have found our own questions, the questions only we can ask ourselves, which in the end are the only questions that matter.

11

Peace comes from knowledge and acceptance of ourselves; knowing what is outside can never destroy our true selves.

12

Peaceful decisions are made from careful reflections and discernment of the heart.

13

Regular periods of silence each day will bring with them an inner and outer wellbeing that radiates peace and joy in the world.

14

Too much speed cancels out peace. When we move at great speed, we are out of touch with our spirit. When we are out of touch with our spirit, peace dissipates.

15

When peace comes into our lives and stillness sets in, there is nothing anyone can do that can destroy or upset our equilibrium.

16

When we are open, the world becomes transparent and we experience with great clarity the interconnectedness of all things.

17

Peace is a gift to be shared, not hoarded.

18

Much of the work we do for peace and justice may not appear successful but our fidelity to it will always triumph.

19

Peace and happiness consists of appreciating what we can so easily take for granted: a fine day, a smile, a kind word.

20

The practice of peace is the most vital and artistic of human actions. A peacemaker is like an artist who creates a painting, a dance, a symphony, a poem. It is the work of a lifetime, a work that permeates all of life.

21

Peacemaking is not an optional extra in life.

22

Morning wakes not only our body but our spiritual being, opening us to all the gifts and graces that await us in this new day.

23

A life lived from the centre of our being is a life of unhurried peace. It is simple. It is serene. It is amazing and radiant.

24

If we choose to live in harmony with ourselves and with nature, we develop a vision of the world as one interacting pattern in which we play a part.

25

Peace is a way of being that calls forth our deepest energies, requiring us to be constantly open to the new, to live from our hearts. It is a practice from which we can never withdraw.

26

The way we approach our day is vital to our peace of mind; it determines whether or not our actions become love made visible or a burden to endure.

27

To be a peacemaker we need to find in our heart a vision for peace that gives meaning and passion to our action.

28

We must find the peace within us before we can appreciate the peace around us.

29

The gospels are all about forgiveness; Jesus forgave everyone. Forgiveness is a gift to pray for.

30

Inner peace makes us wise. When we know what goes on in our own hearts we are more accepting, more tolerant and more open, and we have more respect for the struggles of others.

31

The more peace in us, the more peace there is in the world.

Notes